Penny's Playground

Written by
Lisa Hill
Illustrated by
Earlene Gayle Escalona

To order additional copies of this book, contact:
Xlibris
1-888-795-4274
www.Xlibris.com
Orders@Xlibris.com

Dedicated to my children Michaels Watts Jr., Me'Lisa Watts, Isiah De'Von Horton

Special thanks to my grandmother (Mrs. Delores Smith Johnson), my uncle (Mr. Alonzo Johnson Jr.) loving me enough for rescuing me from an adoption home and training me up the right way and giving me a proper education.

Special acknowledgements to My Big Sister Barbara Theresa Johnson Barnes, Kimberly Scott, Eddie L. Wolfe III, Doris Barnett, Mother Betty Redding, Greg & Carolyn Freeman, Ms. Freemann, all who inspired me to keep praying and don't give up!

ONCE UPON A TIME IN A SMALL TOWN CALLED NEPTUNE, NEW JERSEY. THERE LIVED A LITTLE GIRL NAMED PENNY. NOW PENNY HAD LOTS OF DOLLS AND TOYS TO PLAY WITH INSIDE HER HOME.

BUT PENNY'S FAVORITE TOYS WERE OUTSIDE ON HER PLAYGROUND. A SWING SET WHICH HAD A SWING, SEE-SAW, MONKEY-BARS, AND A SLIDING BOARD.

PENNY WOULD RISE UP EARLY IN THE MORNING BEFORE SCHOOL EAGER TO RUN OUTSIDE TO PLAY ON HER PLAYGROUND.

PENNY'S PLAYRIDE SHE WOULD GET ON WAS HER SWING, THIS WAS HER FAVORITE. SHE WOULD STAY ON THIS RIDE THE LONGEST. BECAUSE THIS RIDE MADE HER FEEL FREE AS A BIRD SWINGING HIGH IN THE BLUE SKIES SINGING HER FAVORITE SONG. JE-SUS LOVES -ME- HE-MAKES- ME- FEEL- FREE-I-FEEL-FREE-BECAUSE-JE-SUS-LOVES-ME!

WEEE- WEEE PENNY GOES AND HAPPY IS SHE!

WHETHER PENNY WAS HAPPY OR SAD HER
PLAYGROUND WAS HER FAVORITE PLACE
TO BE.

WHEN IT WAS RAINING OUTSIDE THIS DID NOT KEEP PENNY FROM ENJOYING HER PLAYGROUND. SHE WOULD PUT ON HER PINK RAINCOAT AND HER PINK BOOTS AND OFF SHE GO RUNNING OUTSDE RUNNING AND SPLASHING WATER ALL AROUND HER PLAYGROUND.

PENNY'S NEXT FAVORITE RIDE WAS HER SEE-SAW SHE LOVED THE WAY THIS RIDE TOOK HER UP REALLY HIGH IN THE SKY AND LANDED HER BACK DOWN GENTLE TO THE GROUND.

THEN PENNYWOULD JUMP ONTO HER MONKEY-BARS. AS SHE WAS SWINGING ON IT UPSIDE DOWN PENNY WOULD SING HER SONG ABOUT HER 1-2-3-'S---1-2-3 I AM FREE, 4-5-6 LOOK AT ME, 7-8-9 I AM SWINGING AND I FEEL FINE-10 WHAT FUN FLYING IN THE WIND.

WHEN PENNY JUMPED DOWN OFF THE MONKEY-BARS SHE CLIMBED UP THE STEPS TO HER SLIDING BOARD AND SAT DOWN TO SLIDE DOWN AND AS SHE WAS SLIDING DOWN SHE RAISED HER HANDS TO THE SKY AND YELLED YEA- YEA I'M FREE NOW IT'S TIME FOR SCHOO-OOL AND I WILL BE BACK SOOOON!

Printed in the United States
by Baker & Taylor Publisher Services